PRAISE GOD FROM WHOM ALL BLESSINGS FLOW
A Sung Prayer of the Christian Tradition

PRAISE GOD FROM WHOM ALL BLESSINGS FLOW
A Sung Prayer of the Christian Tradition

Samuel J. Rogal

The History of Christian Hymnody
Volume 1

The Edwin Mellen Press
Lewiston•Queenston•Lampeter

Library of Congress Cataloging-in-Publication Data

Praise God from whom all blessings flow : a sung prayer of the Christian tradition / Samuel J. Rogal.
     p. cm. -- (The history of Christian hymnody ; v. 1)
  Includes bibliographical references.

ISBN 0-7734-0842-8
  1. Ken, Thomas, 1637-1711. Praise God from whom all blessings flow. 2. Hymns, English--History and criticism. I. Rogal, Samuel J. [II. Title. III. Series.]
  BV317.P73P73 2009
  264'.23--dc22

2009032059

This is volume 1 in the continuing series
History of Christian Hymnody

HCH Series ISBN-13: 978-0-7734-3903-0
HCH Series ISBN-10: 0-7734-3903-X

A CIP catalog record for this book is available from the British Library.

Copyright © 2010 Samuel J. Rogal

All rights reserved. For information contact

    The Edwin Mellen Press   The Edwin Mellen Press
    Box 450   Box 67
    Lewiston, New York   Queenston, Ontario
    USA 14092-0450   CANADA L0S 1L0

The Edwin Mellen Press, Ltd.
Lampeter, Ceredigion, Wales
UNITED KINGDOM SA48 8LT

Printed in the United States of America

Praise God from whom all Blessings flow,
Praise Him all creatures here below,
Praise Him above ye Heavenly Host,
Praise Father, Son, and Holy Ghost.

Table of Contents

Praise God from Whom All Blessings Flow (1693, 1695, 1709)

1. The Texts	1
2. Introduction to the Hymn	10
3. The Text as Poem and as Congregational Hymn	13
4. The Text in Hymn Book and Hymnal	16
5. Thomas Ken (1637-1711): His Life	25
6. Thomas Ken: Hymnodist	29
7. The Hymn Tunes and Their Composers	29
8. Personal Reaction	36
9. List of Works Cited and Consulted	38

THOMAS KEN (1637-1711)

PRAISE GOD FROM WHOM ALL BLESSINGS FLOW (1693, 1695, 1709)

1. The Texts

The oft-recalled and oft-sung doxology[1] of Bishop Thomas Ken--
Praise God from whom all Blessings flow,
Praise Him all creatures here below,
Praise Him above ye Heavenly Host,
Praise Father, Son, and Holy Ghost.--

did not, initially, exist as a separate and distinct piece of hymnody. Rather, those four lines originated as the final stanza to three of Ken's longer hymns: "An Evening Hymn" (1693, 1695, 1709), "A Morning Hymn" (1695, 1709); and "A Midnight Hymn" (1695, 1709). To begin it all, one should note that in the 1674 edition of Bishop Ken's *Manual of Prayers for Winchester College*, there lies the direction to the scholars: "Be sure to sing the Morning and Evening and Midnight Hymn in your chamber devoutly. . . ."--meaning that the three hymns under discussion had been written at least twenty years prior to their having been placed

---

[1] The term "doxology" applies to any form of praise to the Blessed Trinity and assumes two types: (1) that confined to the *Gloria in excelsis*, limited to the Roman Mass and the Anglican Communion service, differing in plainsong according to the feast, and known as the "Greater Doxology"; (2) that which focuses upon the *Gloria Patri*, usually found at the end of paraphrases of Psalms, and identified as the "Lesser Doxology." See John Julian (ed.), *A Dictionary of Hymnology*, 2nd ed., rev. (London: John Murray, 1907; rpt. New York, Dover Publications, Inc., 1957), 1:308-310; Michael Kennedy, *The Oxford Dictionary of Music* (Oxford and New York: Oxford University Press, 1985): 209.

on printed pages.² Further, the various dates assigned to the *publication* of each piece indicate Ken's willingness to revise his work whenever he thought necessary or when the occasion demanded that he do so. Thus, one also needs to consider, before observing the actual texts, the three volumes in which one or more of those hymns *publicly³* appeared: (1) *Harmonia Sacra; or, Divine Hymns and Dialogues. . .Composed by the Best Masters. . .The Words by Several Learned and Pious Persons. The Second. Book* (London: Henry Playford, 1693)-- "An Evening Hymn" only; (2) *A Manual of Prayers for the Use of the Scholars of Winchester College. And All Other Devout Christians. To Which Is Added Three Hymns for Morning, Evening and Midnight* (London: Printed for Charles Brome, 1695); and (3) *A Manual of Prayers for the Use of the Scholars of Winchester College. And All Other Devout Christians. To Which Is Added Three Hymns for Morning, Evening and Midnight. By the Same Author.* Newly Revised (London: Printed for Charles Brome, 1709).

To view the doxology set within its full context, the texts of those hymns now follow;[4] changes (except for spelling, capitalization, and punctuation) indicated in the footnotes:

An Evening Hymn (1693)

[1] All praise[5] to Thee my God this night
For all the blessings of the light;
Keep me, O keep me, King of kings,[6]
Under[7] Thy own Almighty Wings.

[2] Forgive me, Lord, for Thy dear Son,

---

[2] Julian, *Dictionary of Hymnology*, 1:617.
[3] See Section 2 for earlier appearances in print.
[4] Found in Julian, *Dictionary of Hymnology*, 1:618-621.
[5] 1695: "Glory to Thee. . . ."
[6] See Ezekiel 26:7; 1 Timothy 6:15; Revelation 7:14, 19:16-- "And he hath on his vesture and on his thigh a name written, KING OF KINGS, AND LORD OF LORDS." (KJV)
[7] 1709: "Beneath. . . ."

The ill that I this day have done,
That with the world, myself and Thee,
I, ere I sleep, at peace may be.

[3] Teach me to live, that I may dread
The Grave as little as my bed;
Teach me to die, so that[8] I may[9]
Triumphing rise at the last day.[10]

[4] Oh may my soul on Thee repose
And with sweet sleep mine eyelids close,
Sleep that may me more vig'rous make,
To praise[11] my God when I awake.

[5] When in the night I sleepless lie,
My soul with heav'nly thoughts supply;
Let no ill dreams disturb my rest,
No pow'rs of darkness me molest.

[6] My dearest Lord, how am I griev'd
To lye so long of Thee bereaved!
Dull sleep of sence me to deprive,
I am but half my days alive.[12]

[7] But though sleep o'er my weakness[13] reigns,
Let it not hold me long in chains,

---

[8] 1695: "...that so...."
[9] 1709: "To dye, that this vile body may...."
[10] 1709: "Rise glorious at the awful day."
[11] 1695, 1709: "...serve...."
[12] 1695, 1709: Dull sleep of sense me to deprive,
    I am but half my days* alive;
    Thy faithful lovers, Lord, are griev'd
    To lye so long of thee bereav'd.
  *1709: time alive
[13] 1695, 1709: "...frailty...."

Praise God from Whom All Blessings Flow

But[14] now and then let loose my heart,
    Till it an Hallelujah dart;[15]
[8] The faster sleep the sense doth bind,
    The more unfetter'd is the mind;[16]
    Oh may my soul from matter free
    The[17] unveil'd Goodness waking[18] see.
[9] Oh! when shall I in endless day,
    For ever chase dark sleep away,
    And endless praise with th' heavenly[19] choir,
    Incessant sing and never tire.
[10] You my best Guardians, whilst I sleep,
    Close to my bed your vigils keep,
    And in my stead all the night long[20]
    Sing to my God a grateful song.[21]
[11] Praise God from whom all Blessings flow,
    Praise Him all creatures here below,

---

[14] 1695, 1709: "And...."
[15] Dart = come forth swiftly.
[16] 1709: "...are our Minds...."
[17] 1695, 1709: "Thy...."
[18] 1709: "...loveliness unclouded...."
[19] 1709: "...Hymns with the Supernal [heavenly]...."
[20] 1695: "Divine Love into me instill...."
    1709: "His Love Angelical instill...."
[21] 1695, 1709: "Stop all the avenues of ill." Then follows a stanza, the first two lines of each not in the 1693 text:

                      1695
Thought to thought with my soul converse
Celestial joys to me rehearse,
And in my stead all the night long,
Sing to my God a grateful Song.
                      1709
May he Celestials Joys rehearse
And thought to thought with me converse,
Or in my stead all the Night long,
Sing to my God a Grateful Song.

Praise God from Whom All Blessings Flow

Praise Him above the[22] angelick Host,
Praise Father, Son, and Holy Ghost.

A Morning Hymn (1695)

[1] Awake my Soul, and with the Sun,
Thy daily stage of Duty run;[23]
Shake off dull sloth, and early[24] rise,
To pay thy morning Sacrifice.

[2] Redeem thy mis-spent time that's past,[25]
Live this day, as 't were thy last:[26]
T' improve thy Talent take due care,[27]
'Gainst[28] the great Day thy self prepare.

[3] As all thy Converse[29] be sincere,
Thy[30] Conscience as the Noon-day clear;
Think how all-seeing God thy ways,
And all thy secret Thoughts surveys.

[4] Influenc'd by[31] the Light divine,
Let thine own Light in good Works[32] shine:

---

[22] 1695: "...y'...." 1709: "...ye...."
[23] See "The General Prologue" to Geoffrey Chaucer's *The Canterbury Tales* (1386-1400): "... the yonge sonne/Hath in the Ram his halve cours yronne...." (7-8) The Sun has been declared "young" because it has run only half the distance through its course in Ares (the Ram)—that being the first sign in the solar year. Ken's couplet, however, does not attach itself to a specific season of the year.
[24] 1709: "...joyful...."
[25] 1709: "Thy precious time, mis-pent, redeem...."
[26] 1709: "Each present day thy last Esteem...."
[27] 1709: "Improve thy Talent with due Care...."
[28] 1709: "For...."
[29] 1709: "In Conversation...."
[30] 1709: "Keep...."
[31] 1709: "By influence of...."
[32] 1709: "...Light to others...."

Reflect all Heav'n's propitious[33] ways,[34]
In ardent love and chearful [sic] praise.

[5] Wake, and lift up thy self, my Heart,
And with the Angels bear thy part,
Who all night long unwearied sing,
Glory[35] to the Eternal King.

[6] I wake, I wake, ye heavenly Choire,
May your devotion me inspire,
That I like you my Age may spend,
Like you may on my God attend.

[7] May I like you in God delight,
Have all day long my God in sight,
Perform like you my Maker's Will,
O may I never more do ill.

[8] Had I your Wings, to Heaven I'd fly,
But God shall that defect supply,
And my Soul wing'd with warm desire,
Shall all day long to Heav'n aspire.

[9] Glory[36] to Thee who safe hast kept,
And hast refresh't me whilst I slept.
Grant Lord, when I from death shall wake,
I may of endless Light partake.

[10] I would not wake, not rise again,[37]

---

[33] Propitious = favorable, kindly, fortunate.
[34] 1709: "...Rays...."
[35] 1709: "High Praise...."
[36] 1709: "All praise...."
[37] See Jeremiah 51:39, 57— "In their heat I will make their feasts, and I will make them drunken, that they may rejoice, and sleep a perpetual sleep, and not wake, saith the Lord./...and they shall sleep a perpetual sleep, and not wake, saith the King, whose name is the Lord of Hosts." (KJV)

Ev'n[38] Heav'n it self I would disdain;
   Wer't not Thou there to be enjoy'd,
   And I in Hymns to be employ'd.[39]

[11] Heav'n is, dear Lord, where e'er Thou art,
   O never then from me depart;
   For to my soul 't is Hell to be,
   But for one moment without[40] Thee.

[12] Lord I my vows to Thee renew,
   Scatter[41] my Sins as Morning dew,
   Guard my first springs of thought, and will,
   And with thy self my Spirit fill.

[13] Direct, controul, suggest this day,
   All I design, or do, or say;
   That all my Powers with all their might,
   In thy sole Glory may unite.

[14] Praise God from whom all Blessings flow,
   Praise Him all creatures here below,
   Praise Him above y' Angelick[42] Host,
   Praise Father, Son, and Holy Ghost.

A Midnight Hymn (1695)

[1] Lord, now my sleep does me forsake,[43]
   The sole possession of me take,

---

[38] 1709: "And...."
[39] See Ephesians 5:19; Colossians 3:16.
[40] 1709: "...void of...."
[41] 1709: "Disperse...."
[42] 1709: "...ye Heavenly...."
[43] 1709: "My God I now from sleep awake..."

Praise God from Whom All Blessings Flow

Let no vain fancy me illude [sic],[44]

No one impure desire intrude.[45]

[2] Blest Angels! while we silent lye,

You Halleluiahs sing on high,

You, ever wakeful near the Throne,[46]

Prostrate, adore the Three in One.[47]

[3] I now awake do with you[48] joyn,

To praise our God in Hymns[49] divine;

With you in Heav'n I hope to dwell,

And bid the night and world farewell.

[4] My Soul when I shake off this dust,

Lord, in thy Arms I will entrust;

O make me thy peculiar care,

Some heav'nly Mansion me[50] prepare.[51]

[5] Give me a place at thy Saints feet,

Or some fall'n Angel's vacant seat;

I'll strive to sing as loud as they,

Who sit above in brighter day.

[6] O may I always ready stand,

With my Lamp burning in my hand,

May I in sight of Heav'n rejoyce,

---

[44] 1709: "From Midnight Terrors me secure. . . ."
[45] 1709: "And guard my Heart from Thoughts impure."
[46] 1709: "You Joyful Hymns the ever Bless'd. . . ."
[47] 1709: "Before the Throne and never rest."
[48] 1709: "I with your Choir Celestial. . . ."
[49] 1709: "In offering up a Hymn. . . ."
[50] 1709: "Some Mansion for my Soul. . . ."
[51] John 14:2-- "In my Father's house are many mansions; if it were not so, I would have told you. I go to prepare a place for you." (KJV)

When e're I hear the Bridegrooms' voice.[52]

[7] Glory[53] to thee in light array'd,
    Who light thy dwelling place hast made,
    An immense[54] Ocean of bright beams,
    From thy All-glorious Godhead streams.

[8] The Sun, in its Meridian[55] height,
    Is very darkness in thy sight:
    My Soul, O lighten and enflame,
    With Thought and Love of thy great Name.

[9] Blest Jesu, Thou on Heav'n intent,
    Whole nights hast in Devotion spent,
    But I, frail Creature, soon am tir'd,
    And all my Zeal is soon expir'd.

[10] My Soul, how canst thou weary grow,
    Of Antedating[56] Heav'n[57] below,
    In sacred Hymns, and Divine[58] Love,
    Which will eternal be above?[59]

[11] Shine on me Lord, new life impart,
    Fresh ardours[60] kindle in my heart;

---

[52] John 3:29-- "He that hath the bride is the bridegroom: but the friend of the bridegroom, which standeth and heareth him, rejoiceth greatly because of the bridegroom's voice: this my joy therefore is fulfilled." (KJV)

[53] 1709: "All Praise. . . ."

[54] 1709: "A boundless. . . ."

[55] Meridian identifies a circle of constant longitude that passes through a given place and the terrestrial poles (North and South), crossing the Equator at right angles. Further, the term represents a corresponding line on a map or in the sky. In the broadest of contexts--as in the instance of Bishop Ken's "Sun"-- "meridian" means the highest point, or the peak.

[56] To antedate = to set or establish an earlier date on an event or a place.

[57] 1709: ". . .Bliss. . . ."

[58] 1709: ". . .Heav'nly. . . ."

[59] 1709: The sentence ends in the declarative, instead of the 1693 interrogative, mood.

[60] Ardor = intense emotion, passion, enthusiasm, eagerness.

One ray of thy All-quickening light
Dispels the sloth[61] and clouds of night.

[12] Lord, lest the tempter me surprise,
Watch over thine own Sacrifice,
All loose, all idle thoughts cast out,
And make my very dreams devout.

[13] Praise God from whom all Blessings flow,
Praise Him all creatures here below,
Praise Him above y' Angelick[62] Host,
Praise Father, Son, and Holy Ghost.

2. Introduction to the Hymn

At some point between 1893 and 1906, researchers uncovered two additional publications of Bishop Ken's three hymns bearing his doxology. The first, a twelve-page pamphlet, but without a separate title-page, nonetheless yielded a heading on the opening page: *A Morning and Evening Hymn, Formerly Made by a Reverend Bishop*; then followed the "Morning Hymn" in twelve stanzas and the "Evening Hymn" in thirteen stanzas. At the end of it all appeared the statement, "London: printed for Rich[ard]. Smith, Bookbinder, in New-Street, Near Fetter-Lane, 1692." The second pamphlet began not with a title, but with an "Advertisement," informing readers that "The Author finding imperfect and surreptitious Copies of these Hymns printed without his Knowledge and much against his Will, was persuaded to publish them in his own Defence; Otherwise he should not have sent things so very inconsiderable to the Press." Then followed a title, *Three Hymns. By the Author of the Manual of Prayers for the Use of the*

---

[61] Sloth = distaste of physical or mental exertion; overall laziness.
[62] 1709: "...ye Heavenly...."

Scholars of Winchester College.[63] London: Printed for Ch[arles]. Brome, at the Gun, at the West End of St. Paul's Church, 1694. The volume included the "Morning Hymn" (14 stanzas), the "Evening Hymn" (12 stanzas), and the "Midnight Hymn" (13 stanzas).

The most important points to be underscored here focus on the fact that Richard Smith had printed an unauthorized text of Ken's three hymns, forcing Ken to engage Charles Brome in publishing "authorized" versions of those pieces. Smith's texts differ significantly from Ken's originals--the most serious being the omission of the "Doxology" from the "Morning Hymn"; and inserting the "Doxology" into the "Evening Hymn" at stanza 11 of the thirteen stanzas.[64] Of Richard Smith, information relative to his life and vocation remain essentially obscure, which leads to the belief that he carried on his business but for a short time. Charles Brome, however, has been identified as a bookseller who plied his trade, simultaneously, from three different (but not far apart from one another) London locations between 1684 and 1711: the Gun, St. Paul's Churchyard; the West End of St. Paul's Churchyard; and the West End of St. Paul's in Ludgate Street. He succeeded a relative (his mother, perhaps)--Joanna Brome, the widow of Henry Brome--at the Gun in 1684, at which time he published a wide variety of literature, and what appears to have been his final advertisement, in the *Daily Courant* of 2 January 1711, reads, "The four following Books printed for C. Brome at the Gun, the West End of St. Paul's Church: (1) *The Compleat*

---

[63] Founded by the English prelate and statesman, William of Wykeham (1324-1404), in 1382, Winchester College, in Hampshire, stands as one of the oldest public schools in England. By 1678, the number of boys enrolled had reached 127 (fifty of that number being commoners); enrollment would rise to 181 in 1732 and to 186 in 1778. However, the history of Winchester reveals an unwillingness to undertake significant expansion, principally because of its close ties with Oxford University. See Malcolm Seaborne, *The English School: Its Architecture and Organization, 1370-1870* (Toronto: University of Toronto Press, 1971): 56-57, 79, 239-240, 245.

[64] Julian, *Dictionary of Hymnology*, 2:1658-1659. Dr. Julian had examined both the 1692 and 1694 texts: Smith's pamphlet then (1907) in the Hymnological Department of the Church House Library, Westminster; the Brome text in the British Museum, London.

Gamster; (2) *Geographical Cards on Copper plates*; (3) *The Presbyterians, Anabaptists, Independents, Quakers, &c., lively represented on a copper cutt*; (4) *The Dissenters sayings in their own words.*"[65]

Exactly when hymnal compilers and editors detached the "doxology" portion from Ken's "Morning," "Evening," and "Midnight" hymns and placed the four lines in a section apart from the main hymn collection cannot easily be determined. Dr. Julian would only inform his late nineteenth-century readers that, with but few exceptions, "Modern Nonconformist collections [published in Great Britain] generally adopt the practice of giving the doxologies with the hymns. . . .In modern American collections, doxologies are usually appended at the end of the book and represent all the metres contained therein, as in the Protestant Episcopal *Hymnal*, 1871; the Methodist Episcopal *Hymnal*, 1878; [Edwin Francis] Hatfield's *Church Hymn-Book*, 1872; the Baptist *Service of Song*, 1872, and others." Rev. Julian then concluded his discussion with the critical observation that "The provision which has thus been made not only for the holy Seasons of the Church, but also for general purposes, and for the great variety of metre found in modern hymn-books, is very abundant. Where sameness and painful reiteration are unavoidable, it is useless to expect uniform excellence throughout. When, however, the wearisome commonplace is broken by Bp. Ken's 'Praise God, from whom all blessings flow'; [Isaac] Watts's 'Give to the Father praise'; [Edward] Osler's 'Worship, honour, glory, blessing'; or by one of the finer translations from the Latin, we realize that a noble hymn need not be weakened by an ignoble doxology."[66]

---

[65] Henry R. Plomer, *A Dictionary of the Printers and Booksellers Who were at Work in England, Scotland, and Ireland from 1668 to 1725* (Oxford: Oxford University Press, 1922; rpt. London: The Bibliographical Society, 1968): 51. An entry for Richard Smith does not appear in this volume.

[66] *Dictionary of Hymnology*, 1:309-310.

3. The Text As Poem and As Congregational Hymn

Whether one can actually define Bishop Ken's doxology as a "poem" creates an obvious problem when one attempts to discuss those four lines as *poetry*—or even as a congregational hymn, for that matter. What does exist consists, essentially, as a metrical prayer—or, perhaps, as a metrical expression of praise:

> Praise God from whom all Blessings flow,
> Praise Him all creatures here below,
> Praise Him above ye Heavenly Host,
> Praise Father, Son, and Holy Ghost.

The four lines can be comfortably set down inside the confines of a single sentence: *Creatures in both heaven and upon earth must praise the Holy Trinity, the origin of all our blessings.* The poet has extended the sentence by way of repetition—an obvious and often necessary element of prayer. Yet, the true quality of the doxology emerges with the recognition that the four lines stand not only by themselves, but can easily be attached to the end of practically any English hymn that would benefit from such an utterance—as Ken proved in his prayer-hymns "Morning," "Evening," and "Midnight." Note that Charles Wesley's "Hymn for the Kingswood Colliers" (1740), eight four-line stanzas, begins,

> Glory to God, whose sovereign grace
> Hath animated senseless stones,
> Call'd us to stand before His face,
> And raised us into *Abraham's* sons. (1:1-4) --

The piece focuses hard upon the need to accept that

> Thy single arm, Almighty Lord,
> To us the great salvation brought'
> Thy Word, Thy all-creating Word,
> That spake at first the world from nought. (4:1-4)

and it comes to rest upon the understanding that—

> But, O the power of grace Divine!
> In hymns we now our voices raise,
> Loudly in strange hosannas join,
> And blasphemies are turn'd to praise. (8:1-4)

Specifically, the Wesleyan "praise" assumes the sound and the sense of Bishop Ken's doxology:

> Praise God from whom all Blessings flow,
> Praise Him all creatures here below,
> Praise Him above ye Heavenly Host,
> Praise Father, Son, and Holy Ghost. (1-4)[67]

Either Charles Wesley or John Wesley, the latter usually guiding his brother's verse through the press, perceived not only the obvious transition from the eighth stanza of "Hymn for the Kingswood Collier" to Bishop Ken's doxology, but certainly appreciated the added emphasis and specificity that those four lines would provide to the entire exercise of praising the glory of God.

Although, in his discussion of English poets who bowed deeply in the direction of religion for meaning and expression in their work, Professor Hoxie Neale Fairchild refused to discuss congregational hymnody--probably having realized that if he did so, he would, somewhere, still be adding countless volumes to his tome--he did recognize, at least, a need to trace the clear connection between Bishop Ken's religious poetry and his hymnody. Fairchild initially pointed to Ken's poetic introduction to his *Hymns for All the Festivals of the Year* (published in William Hawkins'[68] 1721 four-volume edition of the

---

[67] From "Part II" of the Wesleys' *Hymns and Sacred Poems* (1740), in *The Poetical Works of John and Charles Wesley*, ed. George Osborn (London: Wesleyan-Methodist Conference Office, 1868-1872), 1:287-288.

[68] Hawkins, a London lawyer, proved to have been Bishop Ken's great-nephew and his executor. He had published a biography of Ken in 1713, which he reprinted in the 1721 edition of the

cleric's *Works*)--indicating that for Ken, the word "hymn" represented all forms of divine poetry. In addition, Ken held rigidly to the notion that religious poetry existed as a serious exercise for the pious on behalf of the pious:

> Bless'd Poetry! Immortal Soul refin'd,
>
> Pure Love with bright Illumination joyn'd,
>
> The Spirit lost in an Ecstatick Height,
>
> Imagination soaring out of Sight,
>
> Seraphic Ardour circling in each Vein,
>
> The Majestatick[69] Presence in the Brain,
>
> Inspir'd to make Mankind with Angels vie,
>
> To emulate the Anthems sung on high.[70]

Fairchild further observed that in Ken's view, the singing of praises to God really helped to define the very existence and function of human beings, since "Something like Reason is in Brutes; Mankind,/A Creature hymning God is best defin'd."[71] Although, further in the poem, Ken admitted that his definition, particularly as applied to those of the late seventeenth century expressing disinterest in religion, might prove inaccurate, he nonetheless believed that "a revival of sacred poetry" would contribute significantly to a "reform [of] the irreligion of the times." He further expressed the conviction of "his great hope" that his own poetry would contribute to, and ultimately hasten, the development of such a revival.[72]

Thus, should one be willing to embrace Professor Fairchild's observations and examples, Ken's doxology represents a small but significant portion of his

---

Works.

[69] Majestatic = pertaining to the majesty of God.

[70] Thomas Ken, "Introduction" to *Works*, cited in Hoxie Neale Fairchild, *Religious Trends in English Poetry. Volume I. 1700-1740. Protestantism and the Cult of Sentiment* (New York: Columbia University Press, 1939): 99.

[71] Ken, "Introduction," in Fairchild, *Religious Trends*, 1:99.

[72] Fairchild, *Religious Trends*, 1:99.

attempt to inject serious thought and religious consideration into an extremely concise, rhythmic call to prayer and praise. That the four lines of that doxology have continued to reverberate from the pews of certain Protestant congregations for well over three centuries underscores the claim that, insofar as concerns hymnody and metrical forms of prayer, length--or brevity, in this instance--has little to do with liturgical longevity. Of course, the existence of anti-Trinitarian Protestant religious organizations--the Unitarians, who reject the doctrine of the Trinity and the Divinity of Christ in favor of the "single" personality of God, come immediately to mind-- prevents such a doxology as Ken's "Praise God from whom all blessings flow" from achieving the broadest spheres of possible acceptance. If nothing else, proclaimed the Princetonian Horton Davies, Ken's doxology remains fixed as "a fitting monument to the piety and sensitive consciences of the Non-Juring divines."[73]

4. The Text in Hymn Book and Hymnal

Not surprisingly, there have been, through more than three centuries, attempts to imitate, construct variations upon, and even parody Ken's Doxology, but, overall, such efforts have not endured, nor do they appear worthy of extended discussion. However, before dismissing the entire subject, one ought to devote a moment or two in the pursuit of Charles Wesley's effort in the exercise, as found in his thirty-six-page *Hymns on God's Everlasting Love. To Which Is Added The Cry of a Reprobate and The Horrible Decree* (Bristol: Printed by Samuel and Felix Farley, 1741)--a volume containing eighteen hymns. Under the

---

[73] *Worship and Theology in England. II. From Andrewes to Baxter and Fox, 1603-1690* (Princeton: Princeton University Press, 1975; rpt. Grand Raids, Michigan: William B. Eerdmans Publishing Company, 1996): 283. Non-Jurors comprised those members of the Church of England who, after the "Glorious Revolution" of 1688, refused to swear to the Oath of Allegiance and Supremacy to William III and Mary. They believed that by so dong, they would violate their previous oaths to James II and his successors. As a result, nine bishops (Thomas Ken among them) and four hundred priests lost their livings.

heading "Gloria Patri," the fifth piece reads,

> Praise God from whom pure blessings flow,
> Whose bowels yearn on all below,
> Who would not have one sinner lost;
> Praise Father, Son, and Holy Ghost. (1-4)[74]

Lest the physiologists in the reading audience of this discussion become aroused, Wesley, throughout his verse, relied heavily upon the Biblically-based "bowels," as in Philippians 1:8--"For God is my record, how greatly I long after you all in the bowels of Jesus Christ." (KJV) The meaning of the word, of course, for Wesley and his eighteenth-century contemporaries, focused upon the residence of the deepest and the most tender of emotions--pity, feeling, matters of the heart, *et al*. That issue aside, Wesley, in the second and third lines of his paraphrase of Ken, altered the original so as to provide the recitation with a strong evangelical tone, coming forth, concisely, with the decree that in the work of the evangelical organization known as Methodism, the laborers in and for that enterprise "would not have one sinner lost. . . ."

Other than such relatively few types of, and purposes for, revision, hymnal compilers and hymnal editors have, generally (but not totally), restrained their efforts at textual alteration before pasting Bishop Ken's Doxology upon their pages. Their most significant consideration has been limited to that of the *placement* of the piece within their volumes, rather than a need to adjust the sound or the sense of the text. In England, for example, the editors of *Hymns Ancient and Modern* (1861) first published Ken's "Morning" hymn in two parts; following the final stanza of Part 2 came the directive, "The following Doxology should be used at the end of either Part:"

> Praise God, from Whom all blessings flow,

---

[74] *Poetical Works*, ed. Osborn, 3:100.

Praise Him, all creatures here below,
Praise Him above, ye heav'nly host,
Praise Father, on, and Holy Ghost. Amen.

Then, in their abbreviated version of Ken's "Evening" hymn, they placed, without comment, the Doxology as the sixth and final stanza. The same practice will be found in the third edition (1890) of Edward Henry Bickersteth's *The Hymnal Companion to the Book of Common Prayer*.

Well into the century and following the publication of those two significant Church of England dominated books, in the third edition of another English hymnal, the *Church Hymnary* (1973), a work of 695 hymnodic pieces, five doxologies appear toward the end of the volume: no. 657, "Now to him who loved us," from Samuel Waring's *Sacred Melodies* (1826); no. 658, Ken's "Praise God from whom all blessings flow"; no. 659, "All praise and thanks to God," that being the final stanza of Martin Rinkert's "Now thank we all our God" ("Nun danket alle Gott" [c.1630]), as translated, in 1858, by Catherine Winkworth; no. 660, "Unto God be praise and honour," the final stanza of the Latin hymn "Pange, lingua, gloriosi proelium certaminis" (569 a.d.), by Venatius Honorius Clementianus and translated in *Medieval Hymns* (1851) by John Mason Neale as "Sing, my tongue, the glorious battle"; and no. 661, "Laud and honour to the Father," the last verse of the ninth-century "Angulauris fundamentum laps Christus missus est," also translated by Neale, in this instance for his *Hymnal Noted* (1852-1854). One should note, also, that the editors of this hymnal also included Ken's "Morning" and "Evening" hymns.

A survey of hymnals published in North America yields a variety of practices for the placement of Ken's Doxology. To begin, the editors of the forty-fifth edition (1818) of *The Methodist Hymn Book, Revised and Approved: Designed As a Constant Companion for the Pious of All Denominations* placed Ken's Doxology as the concluding selection, labeling it, simply, "Hymn 320."

Samuel M. Worcester, in the "New Edition" (1834) of *The Psalms, Hymns, and Spiritual Songs of the Rev. Isaac Watts, D.D.*, inserted, as the final section of the book, a collection of nine "Ascriptions,"[75] in which Ken's Doxology appeared as the eighth among those pieces. In *Church Psalmody: A Collection of Psalms and Hymns Adapted to Public Worship* (1841), the piece would have been found as the first of the two identified doxologies that conclude the volume, but nonetheless bears the designation as hymn no. 732. Baron Stow and Samuel Francis Smith, in the "Pew Edition" (1854) of their *The Psalmist: A New Collection of Hymns for the Use of the Baptist Churches*, presented for their worshipers' consideration a section of fourteen doxologies--placed between hymn no. 1180 and the section of "Chants and Selection for Chanting." Bishop Ken's lines headed the list. In their equally comprehensive 1858 edition of *The Sabbath Hymn Book: For the Service of Song in the House of the Lord*, Edwards Amasa Park and Austin Phelps, in Book XV of this large volume (944 pages), included twenty-four doxologies. Bishop Ken's "Praise God, from whom all blessings flow" stood as the second selection.

In 1878, the editors of the *Hymnal of the Methodist Episcopal Church*, although including Ken's "Morning" and "Evening" hymns, excluded the stanza "Praise God from whom all blessing flow" from both texts. Instead, they transferred those lines to the section of "Doxologies" and placed it first among the group of nineteen selections. A totally different approach to the piece, as well as its placement, will be found in the 1895 *Gospel Hymns Nos. 1 to 6*, edited by Ira David Sankey, James McGranahan, and George G. Stebbins. The first page of that volume contains four pieces--all of them set to Louis Bourgeois' version of "Old Hundred": No. 1, William Kethe's four-stanza "All people that on earth do

---

[75] In a strictly ecclesiastical context, an "ascription" referred to a passage *ascribing* praise to God, and initially intended to be spoken or recited by the minister following the sermon. One can readily appreciate the close relationship between the meanings and functions of "ascription" and "doxology."

dwell"; No. 2, Thomas Ken's "Doxology"; No. 3, headed "Grace" ("May be sung before and after meat"), "Be present at our table, Lord," by John Cennick; and No. 4 (under the heading "Thanks Returned"), "We thank Thee, Lord, for this our food," again by Cennick.

Bishop Ken's "Praise God, from Whom all blessings flow" stands as the sixth of thirty-nine doxologies grouped at the very end of Harriet Reynolds Krauth's *Church Book, for the Evangelical Lutheran Congregations* (1897)--all of those pieces huddled together under the editorial directive, "The Amen should always be added to the end of the Doxology, and sung with it, as its proper conclusion." R. H. Boyd, editor of the fourth edition (1906) of *The National Baptist Hymn Book*, placed his ten-piece "Doxologies" section at the outset of the volume, with "Praise God, from whom all blessings flow," as the second offering. The nineteen doxologies of the ninth edition of the *Evangelical Lutheran Hymnal* (1910?), also the last of the hymnal section of the book, have been grouped into three sections--Iambic, Trochaic, and Dactylic[76]-- Ken's doxology being the third in the Iambic section and third overall. Also at the beginning of the contextual range, O. Hardwig's 1918 *Wartburg Hymnal* contains fifteen "Closing" hymns (nos. 12-26), with Ken's four lines appearing as No. 25. Selections Nos. 910-927 of the 952-piece *Hymnal and Liturgies of the Moravian Church* (1920), comprising the section identified as "Doxologies and Benedictions," finds Ken's lines placed seventh in order (No. 916). In their *University Hymns* (1924), Harry B. Jepson and Charles R. Brown provided congregations with two opportunities to render Bishop Ken's "Praise God form whom all blessings flow: (1) as the fifth (and final) stanza of his evening hymn, "All praise to Thee, my God, this night"

---

[76] (1) The *iambus* consists of a metrical foot with one short or unstressed, syllable followed by one long or stressed syllable; an *iambic* line reads, "Praise God from whom all blessings flow." (2) The *trochee*, another metrical foot, consists of one long or stressed syllable followed by one short or unstressed syllable; the *trochaic* line reads, "Praise the name of God most high." (3) the *dactyl* comprises a metrical foot of three syllables, the first stressed and the second and third unstressed. The *dactylic* line will read, "O Father Almighty, to Thee be addressed."

(No. 22), and then separately (No. 24), as the first of seven pieces for "Sunday." That arrangement appears in reverse order in the 1987 *Worship His Majesty*, wherein the editors placed the doxology alone as hymn No. 109, then repeated it later as the fourth and final stanza of Ken's evening hymn (No. 329).

The editors of *The Hymnal of the Protestant Episcopal Church* (1933) did not separate Ken's doxology from its parental text, preferring, instead to leave those four lines as the final stanza of both the morning hymn ("Awake my soul, and with the sun") and the evening hymn ("All praise to Thee, my God this night"). That identical practice will be found in the 2007 *Harvard University Hymn Book* (Nos. 43, 57). Those who compiled the 1997 *The Book of Praise* for the Presbyterian Church of Canada followed the same procedure, except that they also set the final stanza of both hymns separately, as the familiar doxology. However, the editors of the 1933 Presbyterian *The Hymnal*, Clarence Dickinson and Calvin Weiss Laufer, removed those four lines from the two hymns and situated them at the very end of the book, under the heading "Ancient Hymns and Canticles"--the same, essentially, as it appeared in the 1935 *The Methodist Hymnal*, where the heading bears the label "Responses: Doxologies"; in the *Broadman Hymnal* (1940), where the worshiper locates the text beneath "Aids to Worship: Doxology"; in *The Lutheran Hymnal* (1941) entitled, simply, "Praise God, from Whom All Blessings Flow"; in the 1941 *The Hymnal of the Evangelical and Reformed Church* (1941), as the first piece among the "Doxologies and Amens"; in the 1941 *Christian Worship. A Hymnal*, within the section "Doxology, Glorias"; and in the *Book of Worship for United States Forces* (1974) as part of the section of "Offertory Responses and Doxologies."

In *Services of Religion for Use in the Churches of the Free Spirit* (1937), the names of the hymn tunes function as the titles for the poetry. Thus, six pieces

(Nos. 497-502) have been grouped under "Old Hundredth. L.M."[77] and appear in this order: William Kethe's "All people that on earth do dwell" (1561); "Be thou, O God! Exalted high" (1696), from the "New Version" of Nahum Tate and Nicholas Brady; Isaac Watts' "From all that dwell below the skies" (1718); Bishop Ken's "Doxology"; the anonymously written "Praise God the love we all may share" a piece by Gerhard Tersteegen and translated into English by John Wesley in 1739 as "Lo, God is here! Let us adore"; and a 1935 arrangement by Curtis W. Reese that begins "'From all that dwell below the skies."

A commercial, non-denominational hymn collection published in 1947 under the title *Devotional Hymns* (Chicago: Hope Publishing Company) offered worshippers a most unusual placement for Bishop Ken's "Doxology": No. 307 of its 310 selections exists as an addendum to the four stanzas of William Kethe's "All people that on earth do dwell"; following the final stanza, unnumbered and in italics, one finds Ken's four lines. However, editors of other "for profit" volumes simply followed the practice of "main-line" denominational hymnal editors by placing "Praise God from Whom all blessings flow" toward or at the end of their books: the Rodeheaver Company's *Church Service Hymns* (1948), 434 of the 448 selections found therein; Hope Publishing Company's *The Worshiping Church* (1991), Nos. 808-809 within a total of 845 hymns; the 1997 *The Celebration Hymnal* (Word Music/Integrity Music), Nos. 814-815 of a total of 818 hymnodic pieces. That organizational pattern has been broken by the editors of the 1993 *Sing to the Lord* (Lillenas Publishing Company), who began their collection with a paraphrase of Psalms 95:1-7; followed by Reginald Heber's "Holy, holy, holy!

---

[77] L.M. = long metre or long measure: a quatrain in iambic tetrameter lines, with the second and fourth lines definitely rhyming, and lines one and three doing so on most instances. Thus, consider this piece (1561) by William Kethe—
    All people that on earth do dwell,
    Sing to the Lord with cheerful voice;
    Him serve with mirth, His praise forth tell,
    Come ye before Him and rejoice. (1:1-4)

Lord God Almighty" (1826), the anonymous eighteenth-century piece, "Come, Thou Almighty King," and Donna Adkins' "Father we love you" (1976); a paraphrase of Psalms 98:1-4; then, as Nos. 6-7, Ken's "Praise God from Whom all blessings flow." Finally (at least in terms of this brief survey), the editors of a book entitled *Favorite Hymns of Praise* (1967)--either striving for the ultimate in congregational convenience or simply in an effort to save space--affixed the Quam Dilecta (George Root's "The Lord is in His holy temple"), Ken's doxology, the Gloria Patri, and a brief piece for the Offering ("All things come of Thee, O Lord") directly to the inside of the pasteboard cover.

As one wends his or her way out of the chronological and hymnodic twentieth century, there emerges the discovery--although to no one's significant surprise--of efforts to "modernize" Bishop Ken's text. For example, the 1989 *The United Methodist Hymnal* provides two versions, the first of which comprises a 1978 adaptation by Gilbert H. Vieira:

> Praise God from whom all blessings flow;
> praise God, all creatures here below:
> Alleluia! Alleluia!
> Praise God, the source of all our gifts!
> Praise Jesus Christ whose power uplifts!
> Praise the Spirit, Holy Spirit!
> Alleluia! Alleluia! Alleluia!

For the second version of the piece, the editors simply revert to Ken's original text. In *A New Hymnal for Colleges and Schools* (1992), another recasting of Ken's doxology, this by Brian Wren in 1989 (and admittedly "based on Thomas Ken") *follows* the 1674 text and reads:

> Praise God from whom all blessings flow;
> praise God, all creatures high and low:
> Alleluia, alleluia!

Praise God from Whom All Blessings Flow

> Praise God in Jesus fully known;
> Creator, Word, and Spirit One:
>> Alleluia, alleluia,
>> alleluia, alleluia,
>> alleluia!

Although the 2001 *African American Heritage Hymnal* includes Ken's four lines as a doxology (No. 651), its editors precede that setting with a mosaic, of sorts, that joins Ken to fragments from Isaac Watts, and William Kethe--all of it emerging, in No. 650, as:

> [1] Praise God from whom all blessings flow,
> Praise Him all creatures here below,
> Praise Him above ye heavenly host,
> Praise Father, Son, and Holy Ghost.
>
> [2] People and realms of every tongue
> Dwell on His love with sweetest song,
> To Him shall endless prayer be made,
> And endless praises crown His head.
>
> [3] Sing to the Lord with cheerful voice,
> Come ye before Him and rejoice,
> All people that on earth do dwell,
> Serve Him with mirth, His praises tell.

Before departing from this subject, perhaps one should take note, with the same degree of interest as the placement of Ken's Doxology in various hymnals, of those "rare" volumes of congregational song wherein the piece has been excluded from the contents. Thus, for instance, one will not find "Praise God from whom all blessings flow"--or anything else by Thomas Ken, for that matter-- in such collections as the 1932 *Christian Science Hymnal*. In that book, the editors preferred to follow the praises of Tate and Brady and Isaac Watts rather than the lines of Thomas Ken.

5. Thomas Ken (1637-1711): His Life

A native of Little Berkhamstead, Hertfordshire, and the son of Thomas Ken the elder, an attorney there and one firmly attached to the Church of England, young Thomas Ken, following the death of his parents, matured under the guardianship of his brother-in-law (married to his half-sister), the prose writer Izaak Walton (1593-1683), receiving his formal education at Winchester College, Hampshire (1651), and at Hart Hall, Oxford, eventually (1657) holding a fellowship at New College (B.A. 1661). Following ordination into Holy Orders of the Church of England in 1661, Ken maintained the pulpit at Little Easton (1663) and served as chaplain (1665) to Bishop George Morley (1597-1684) of Winchester; he became a fellow of Winchester College (1666), during which time he prepared his *Manual of Prayers for the Use of the Scholars of Winchester College* (1674), an attempt to counteract the unstructured Puritan influence of that institution. Ken further held clerical appointments at Brightstone (or Brixton), on the Isle of Wight (1667)--where he wrote the majority of his hymns--and at Woodhay; he rose to the prebendary[78] stall of Winchester (1669) and received the appointment from Charles II as chaplain to the Princess Mary at the Hague (1679). Having encountered the displeasure of the Princess's husband over the issue of perceived immorality of a marriage within the Dutch court of William of Orange, he returned to Hampshire in 1680 as chaplain to Charles II and eventually succeeded as Bishop of Bath and Wells in 1685.

Ken, one of five bishops at the deathbed of Charles II, administered absolution to the sovereign and read the "Prayers for the Sick" from the Book of

---

[78] Prebendary = a member of the Church of England clergy associated with a cathedral or collegiate church. During Ken's day, the appointment carried with it a living, as well as the revenues from one of the manors of the cathedral estates. By the nineteenth century, however, the office of prebendary had become strictly honorary.

Common Prayer.[79] He also marched to the gallows with the condemned Duke of Monmouth, and, in general, presented himself to the world as the model of Christian virtue. As one of the seven bishops who refused to read to his congregations the Declaration of Indulgence at the command of James II, Ken would not swear allegiance (by way of the Coronation Oath) to William III and Mary, the latter act resulting in imprisonment in the Tower of London (1688) and deprivation of his see (1691). For the remainder of his years, having received a pension of £200 per annum from Queen Anne, Ken endured an ascetic and celibate retirement, refusing an offering of re-instatement to his see in 1703. He died at Longleat, Somersetshire, on 19 March 1711, in the home provided for him by his friend, Lord Viscount Weymouth. In his will, he declared, "I die in the Holy Catholic and Apostolic Faith, professed by the whole Church, before the disunion of East and West: more particularly, I die in the communion of the Church of England, as it stands distinguished from all Papal and Puritan innovations."[80] Among the most noted of Ken's contemporaries, the poet and dramatist John Dryden (1631-1700), the bishop emerged as the model for all clerics, as one who,

> Letting down the golden chain from high,
> He drew his audience upwards to the sky:
> And oft with holy hymns he charmed their ears;
> (A music more melodious than the spheres:)
> For David left him, when he went to rest,
> His lyre: and after him he sung the best.

---

[79] Stephen Coote, *Royal Survivor: A Life of Charles II* (New York: St. Martin's Press, 2000): 349-350.
[80] See *Dictionary of National Biography* (*DNB*), 30:399-404; *The Oxford Dictionary of the Christian Church*, 2nd ed., ed. F.L. Cross and E. Livingstone (Oxford: Oxford University Press, 1974):776; Davies, *Worship and Theology in England. II*, 397-398. Edward Hayes Plumptre's two-volume biography of Ken (London, 1888; 2nd ed. 1890) remains the standard work on the subject, while one would do well to consult Edward Marston's *Thomas Ken and Isaac Walton* (London, 1908).

With considerably less embellishment, the Victorian biographer and literary historian Richard Monkton Milnes, Baron Houghton (1809-1895) offered these lines as tribute upon Ken's tomb:

> These signs of him that slumbers there
>
>   The dignity broken;
>
> These iron bars a heart declare
>
>   Hard bent, but never broken;
>
> This form portrays how souls like his
>
>   Their pride and passion quelling,
>
> Preferred to earth's high palaces
>
>   This calm and narrow dwelling.[81]

According to Rev. Samuel Wesley the elder (1662-1735), in his *A Letter to a Curate* (1709, 1735), "Bishop Ken made almost all who heard him preach begin to weep."[82] Ken, on the other hand, directed the language of his sermon texts to more practical theological issues, such as arguing, with the utmost directness and clarity, for the retention of traditional Christian feasts: For example, in Bishop Ken's view, the purpose of Lent focused upon Christians identifying themselves with Christ in His sorrows and Resurrection, since "a devout soul. . .fastens himself to the Cross on Ash Wednesday, and hangs crucified by contrition all the Lent long." In that particular state, he will arrive at a complete understanding of all of the anguish and deprivation "which God incarnate endured when He bled upon the Cross for the sins of the world; that being purified of repentance and made conformable to Christ crucified, he may

---

[81] Both excerpts quoted in R.E. Welsh and F.G. Edwards, *Romance of Psalter and Hymnal: Authors and Composers* (London: Hodder and Stoughton, 1889):168.

[82] Luke Tyerman, *The Life and Times of the Rev. Samuel Wesley, A.M., Rector of Epworth* (London: Simpkin, Marshall and Company, 1866): 34. 115, 169, 171, 385. See, also, for a survey of Ken's poetic influence upon both Charles and John Wesley, Samuel J. Rogal, *A Biographical Dictionary of Eighteenth-Century Methodism* (Lewiston, New York: The Edwin Mellen Press, 1997-1999), 3:110-113.

offer up a pure oblation[83] at Easter and feel the power and the joys and triumph of Saviour's Resurrection."[84] The London diarist John Evelyn (1620-1706) heard Ken preach on 10 March 1687 at King's Chapel, Whitehall, in London, before a large audience that included the Princess of Denmark and at least thirty members of the nobility, on John 8:46.[85] Ken described "through his whole discourse the blasphemies, perfidy,[86] wresting[87] of Scripture, preference of tradition before it, spirit of persecution, superstition, legends and fables of the Scribes and Pharisees, so that all the auditory[88] understood his meaning of a parallel between them and the Romish[89] priests, and their new Trent religion.[90] He exhorted his audience to adhere to the written Word, and to persevere in the Faith taught in the Church of England, whose doctrine for Catholic and soundness he preferred to all the communities and churches of Christians in the world; concluding with a kind of prophecy, that whatever it suffered, it should after a short trial emerge to the confusion of her adversaries and the Glory of God."[91]

Aside from his hymnodic work, miscellaneous poems, various sermons, and the *Manual of Prayers*, Bishop Ken authored an *Exposition on the Church*

---

[83] Oblation = the offering of gift or a sacrifice to the deity; the offering of bread and wine to God during the Christian service of Communion.
[84] From *A Sermon Preached at the King's Chapel at Whitehall in the Year 1685*, quoted in Davies, *Worship and Theology in England*. II, 226. See John Evelyn's comments upon a later sermon at King's Chapel quoted below.
[85] John 8:46--"Which of you convinceth me of sin? And if I say the truth, why do ye not believe me?" (KJV)
[86] Perfidy = treachery or deceit.
[87] Wrest = to gain or to seize power from an idea, a person, or a text.
[88] Auditory = listeners.
[89] Romish = Roman Catholic.
[90] The Council of Trent (1545-1563) assembled at Trentino, in northern Italy, to undertake a series of reforms by the Roman Catholic Church intended to counter the effects of the Protestant Reformation. Essentially and generally, the work of the assembly established a firm basis for the renewal of discipline and the spiritual life within the Roman Catholic Church, highlighted by a clearly formulated doctrinal system, a strengthened authority for the papacy, and an enhanced religious vigor with which to engage in its continued struggle with Protestantism. See *Oxford Dictionary of the Christian Church*, 2nd ed., 1392-1393.
[91] *The Diary of John Evelyn*, ed. William Bray (1907; rev. 1952; rpt. London: J.M. Dent and Sons, Ltd./Everyman's Library, 1966), 2:266.

Catechism; or, the Practice of Divine Love (1685); a volume dedicated to and bearing the title *The Retired Christian Exercised in Divine Thoughts and Heavenly Meditations for the Closet: With a Suitable Prayer for Each Meditation* (1699; three editions through 1737); and *Directions for Prayer for the Diocese of Bath and Wells* (pub. 1707).

6. Thomas Ken: Hymnodist

Beyond the hymns for morning, evening, and midnight, and the four-line Doxology that concludes each, at least six other hymnodic pieces, published posthumously in *Hymns for All the Festivals of the Year* (1721), achieved short-lived acceptance by the congregations: "All human succours now are flown," for the visitation of the sick; "I had one only thing to do," under the title "A New Creature"; "O purify my soul from stain," to be sung on the sixteenth Sunday after Trinity, or as a "Prayer for Purity"; "O Lord, when near the appointed hour," for Holy Communion; "Our Father, throned in heaven, Thy name be praised," as a for of Lord's Prayer; and "Unction the Christian name implies," for Confirmation. In addition, portions of a separate poem by Ken, "Sion; or, Philothea," have yielded at least two congregational hymns constructed by other hands: "Her Virgin eyes saw God incarnate born" and "When she to Bethlem came that happy morn." However, as indicated above, Thomas Ken's hymnodic legacy rests squarely and solidly upon his "Morning" and "Evening" hymns and, perched above those, his four-line doxology.[92]

7. The Hymn Tunes and Their Composers

The tune "Old One Hundredth" continues to stand as the dominant musical setting for Thomas Ken's doxology, although musicologists have not always

---

[92] See Julian, *Dictionary of Hymnology*, 1:621-622; 2:874, 1647, 1658-1659.

embraced, with total confidence, the actual composer of that piece. For instance, at the beginning of the twentieth century, the view emerged that "This grand Gregorian harmony has been claimed to be [Martin] Luther's production, while some have believed that Louis Bourgeois, editor of the French *Genevan Psalter*, who perished in the Massacre of St. Bartholomew,[93] composed the tune, but the weight of evidence seems to indicate that it was the work of Guillaume le Franc, (William Franck or William the Frenchman,) of Rouen, in France, who founded a music school in Geneva, 1541."[94] Such vague language as "has been claimed to be," "some have believed," and the "weight of evidence seems" clouds those comments with doubt. Commentators during the last quarter of the twentieth century did not really clarify matters when, for example, they declared, with a corporate note of timidity, that "Old 100th was composed or adapted by Louis Bourgeois of Ps[alm]. 134 in *The French Psalter*, 1551."[95] Did Bourgeois compose it, or did he adapt it from the work of another hand--say that of Le Franc? Michael Kennedy, in 1985, traced an early form of the tune to the collection *Souter Liederkens* (Antwerp, 1540), but he did not occupy sufficient textual space to commit himself to the identification of a composer.[96] Nonetheless, "Old One Hundred" remains as the standard setting for Ken's Doxology, although one will note, within the course of this discussion, additional attempts to provide different musical settings for the piece.

For those who wish to consider Guillaume Le Franc (1505?-1570), that composer belonged to a French Protestant family that fled its native Rouen for

---

[93] The St. Bartholomew's Day massacre refers to the murder of over three thousand Protestants at the hands of a Catholic mob at Paris during the night of 23-24 August 1572--the assaults having been ordered by the French queen mother, Catherine de' Medici. Additional deaths occurred throughout the French provinces, and thus the death toll could well have reached fifty thousand.

[94] Theron Brown and Hezekiah Butterworth, *The Story of Hymns and Tunes* (New York: American Tract Society, 1906):15.

[95] John M. Barkley (ed.), *Handbook to the Church Hymnary. Third Edition [1973]* (London and Oxford: Oxford University Press, 1979): 77.

[96] *The Oxford Dictionary of Music* (Oxford and New York, 1985): 514.

Geneva in 1541 to avoid persecution. In that year, Le Franc obtained a license to establish a school of music, and a year later he became a master of the children and a singer at St. Peter's Church. In 1545, principally over a salary dispute, he left Geneva for Lausanne where he joined the choir of the Cathedral of that city-- and where he remained until his death in June 1570. His name and musical reputation has been associated with the later editions of the Psalter published, initially in 1542, at Geneva for the Reformed churches by John Calvin. Originally limited to thirty-five psalms, that book gradually increased in the quantity of selections until its completion in 1562. Although early historians of that work believed Le Franc to have been the music editor, later researchers have discounted that claim--particularly since he had no connection with the Psalter after he left Geneva in 1545. The Council of Geneva might have intended to employ Le Franc to set certain of the psalms to music, but there exists no evidence that the latter actually performed such exercises.

What does come forth as fact concerns Le Franc's efforts, beginning at Lausanne in 1552, to edit a new Psalter that he planned to print at Geneva-- Lausanne having no printing press of its own. Unfortunately, the project never reached the printed stage--only the license of 28 July 1552 survives. Not until 1565 did Le Franc produce his own "Lausanne Psalter," with texts by the French Court poet Clement Marot (1495?-1544) and the French Protestant theologian Theodore de Beze (1519-1605); Le Franc composed or adopted twenty-seven melodies for that volume to Psalms 51, 53, 62, 63, 64, 65, 66, 67, 68, 70, 71, 76, 77, 78, 82, 95, 98, 100, 108, 109, 11, 116, 127, 139, 140, 142, and 144. The "Lausanne Psalter" really existed as a local book, and, shortly following its publication, it fell by the hymnodic wayside in favor of the earlier 1562 Geneva Psalter edited by Louis Bourgeois.[97]

---

[97] *Grove's Dictionary of Music and Musicians*, 3rd ed., ed. H.C. Coles (New York: The Macmillan Company, 1944), 2:291-292.

A native of Paris, Bourgeois (1510?-1561?), Bourgeois, who had been trained as a church musician, remained relatively quiet upon the sixteenth-century French musical scene until 1541, at which time he removed to Geneva--most likely by invitation from either the town magistrates or the church council. When Guillaume Le Franc departed Geneva for Lausanne in 1545, Bourgeois and a Genevan named Guillaume Fabri replaced him at St. Peter's Church--each earning one-half of Le Franc's former salary. On 3 December 1551, the Council of Geneva ordered Bourgeois to prison for having, without permission, altered the tunes of a number of Psalms, but John Calvin rose to the musician's defense and the former gained his release on the day following--and, eventually, the Council accepted those very same adaptations. Ever the innovator, Bourgeois suggested the suspension of a printed table in the churches of Geneva to indicate to the congregation the specific Psalms to be sung, in order, during the service. Even though that suggestion earned him a stipend, he ran afoul of Church authorities over his attempts to introduce part-singing into public worship. Thus, he left Geneva in 1557 and returned to Paris. Practically nothing remains in the way of details of his life after 1561.

Bourgeois' principal claim to recognition lies in his connection with the publication of the completed Geneva Psalter of 1562--a project in which various portions of the volume had emerged from the press, respectively, in 1542, 1543, 1551, 1554, and 1562. Although, during the seventeenth, eighteenth, and nineteenth centuries, considerable controversy had developed as to the authorship of the melodies for that collection, the debate has, essentially, come to an end and various archives at Geneva clearly have revealed that the task of selecting and arranging the tunes had been entrusted to and carried forth by Louis Bourgeois between 1542 and 1557. After departing Geneva for Paris in 1557, Bourgeois severed his connection with the Genevan Psalter; the forty new psalm tunes that appeared in the 1562 Psalter had been added by another, less skilful hand--

reportedly a singer by the name of Pierre Dubuisson. In 1547, at Lyons, there had appeared in print a volume under the title *Pseaulmes Cinquante de David Roy et Prophete, Traduictz en Vers Françoise par Clement Marot, et Mis en Musique par Loys Bourgeoys a Quatre Parties, a Voix de Contrepoinct Egal Consonnante au Verbe. Tousiors Mord Envie*. This volume reportedly encompassed the entire range of Bourgeois' work on the Psalms to the date of publication--although scholars cannot conclude without doubt whether Bourgeois composed all of the melodies, or if he simply arranged them in four-part harmony.[98]

In his discussion of Bishop Ken's "Evening," "Morning," and "Midnight" hymns, each concluding with the Doxology, Dr. Julian stated that the 1695 text of "An Evening Hymn" had been "set by Clarke as a Cantata for a solo voice, with the Doxology as a chorus in four parts."[99] That comment referenced Jeremiah Clarke (1670?-1707), a native of London who began his music career as a chorister in the Chapel Royal under the noted composer and organist John Blow (1649-1708). Clarke served as organist at Winchester College (1692-1695)--and thus his direct connection with Thomas Ken. He also succeeded, in 1693, Blow as almoner[100] and master of the children at St. Paul's Cathedral, London, followed by an appointment, two years later, as organist of St. Paul's--and eventually (1705) to the position as vicar-choral there. Then, in July 1700, Clarke and his colleague, William Croft (1678-1727) took the oaths as gentlemen-extraordinary of the Chapel Royal, with the provision that should the position of organist extraordinary fall vacant, both would assume that post. That event occurred in May 1704 upon the death of Francis Piggott, and both Clarke and Croft succeeded him. Unfortunately for Clarke, he became infatuated with an unidentified woman whose higher social position in life rendered his union with her virtually

---

[98] *Grove's Dictionary of Music and Musicians*, 3rd ed., 1:433-435; Barkley, *Handbook to the Church Hymnary*, 231.
[99] *Dictionary of Hymnology*, 1:618.
[100] The almoner attended to the general welfare of the pupils in his charge.

impossible. Thus, the musician fell into a state of complete despondency, under the influence of which he shot himself at his house in St. Paul's Churchyard, the incident having been uncovered by his friend, John Reading (1677-1764), then the organist of St. Dunstan's Church. Clarke's compositions included anthems (the most notable being "Ode on the Glorious Assumption of the Blessed Virgin" and "Praise the Lord, O Jerusalem"), songs, and music for the opera and the dramatic stage.[101]

Consider, finally, this "musical" summary of selected hymn collections and hymnals that include Thomas Ken's Doxology, arranged by the tunes to which the piece has been set:

COME TOGETHER:[102] *The Book of Praise* (1997).

DUKE STREET (Elvey): *Sing to the Lord* (1993).[103]

DUKE STREET (Hatton):[104] *African American Heritage Hymnal* (2001).[105]

FAIRHILL (1972):[106] *The Celebration Hymnal* (1997).

LASST UNS ERFREUN:[107] *The United Methodist Hymnal* (1989); *Sing to the Lord* (1993).

OLD HUNDREDTH: *Gospel Hymns Nos. 1 to 6 Complete* (1895); O.

---

[101] *Grove's Dictionary of Music and Musicians*, 3rd ed., 1:658-659; Kennedy, *The Oxford Dictionary of Music*, 149; Charles Burney, *A General History of Music, from the Earliest Ages to the Present Period [1789]*, ed. Frank Mercer (New York: Dover Publications, Inc., 1957), 2:475-476. "The anthems of this pathetic composer," wrote Burney of Jeremiah Clarke, ". . .are natural and pleasing. . .wholly free from licentious harmony and breach of rule. He is mild, placid, and seemingly incapable of violence of any kind." (476)

[102] By Jimmy Owens (1930-?); arrangement by David Peacock (1949-?).

[103] Listed as an alternate tune for Ken's Doxology. "Duke Street" written in 1868 by the organist of St. George's Chapel, Dr. Sir George Job Elvey (1816-1893).

[104] Composed by John Hatton (1710?-1793), who resided in St. Helens, Buckinghamshire, in the township of Windle, and on the street from which his tune derives its name.

[105] As indicated by the editors of this hymnal, Hatton's "Duke Street" underwent adaptation by one George Coles, with an arrangement, in 1968, by Roberta Martin (1912-1968).

[106] By Jimmy Owens (1930-?); copyright held by Bud John Songs, Inc., Brentwood, Tennessee.

[107] From the *Geistliche Kirchengesanglinge* (1623), with the harmony provided (1906) by the English composer, conductor, and organist Ralph Vaughan Williams (1872-1958).

Hardwig, *Wartburg Hymnal* (1918);[108] *Hymnal and Liturgies of the Moravian Church* (1920);[109] *University Hymns* (1924);[110] *The Hymnal of the Presbyterian Church* (1933); *The Hymnal of the Protestant Episcopal Church* (1933); *The Methodist Hymnal* (1935); *Services of Religion* (1937); *The Broadman Hymnal* (1940); *Christian Worship* (1941); *The Hymnal of the Evangelical and Reformed Church* (1941); *The Lutheran Hymnal* (1941); *Devotional Hymns* (1947); *Church Service Hymns* (1948); *Favorite Hymns of Praise* (1973); *The Church Hymnary* (1973); *Book of Worship for United States Forces* (1974); *Worship His Majesty* (1987); *The United Methodist Hymnal* (1989); *The Worshiping Church* (1990); *A New Hymnal for Colleges and Schools* (1992); *Sing to the Lord* (1993); *The Book of Praise* (1997);[111] *The Celebration Hymnal* (1997); *African American Heritage Hymnal* (2001).

PORT JERVIS (1967):[112] *Book of Worship for United States Forces* (1974).

WITHOUT TUNE: Lowell Mason and David Greene, *Church Psalmody* (1831); Samuel Worcester, *Psalms, Hymns, and Spiritual Songs of the Rev. Isaac Watts* (1834); Baron Stow and Samuel Francis Smith, *The Psalmist* (1843, 1854); Edwards Amasa Parks and Austin Phelps, *The Sabbath Hymn Book* (1858); *Hymnal of the Methodist Episcopal Church* (1878); *Church Book, for the Use of Evangelical Lutheran Congregations* (1897); R.H. Boyd, *The National Baptist*

---

[108] Authorship of tune assigned to "G. Franc."
[109] Although music notations not included for "Doxologies and Benedictions," Ken's piece headed "The Old Hundredth," with a reference to the music for John Wesley's adaptation of Isaac Watts' "Before Jehovah's glorious throne."
[110] Tune source identified as "Pseaumes Octante Trois, 1551."
[111] The final line of the music from *The Whole Booke of Psalmes, with the Hymnes Evangelical and Songs Spiritual, with the Music Composed into Four Parts by Sundry Authors* (1621), by the English composer and music publisher Thomas Ravenscroft (1592?-1635).
[112] Composed by Richard K. Avery (1934-?) and Donald S. Marsh (1925-?); an arrangement of this tune by Thomas W. Holcombe (1943-?). The tune derives its name from Port Jervis, Orange County, New York, on the Delaware River, thirty-eight miles west of Newburgh., and settled in 1698.

Hymn Book (1906); *Evangelical Lutheran Hymnal* (1910?).

8. Personal Reaction

In a somewhat indirect route to the proving of a point, the Princeton academician and hymnologist Louis Fitzgerald Benson once lectured on the fact that "*The Hymn at the Opening of Service* deserves more attention than it gets from pastors. It is psychologically important. The custom of opening [the service] with the L.M.[113] doxology came down from New England, whence I fear the custom of sitting at prayer also came. In its own way it is equally inept. The doxology used to be the Te Deum[114] of the unliturgical; reserved for occasion, sung with feeling. What has cheapened it and taken the heart out of it is the simple psychological truth that the late breakfast and scanning the Sunday newspaper and the rush to be in time for church do not lay an adequate foundation for so lofty a burst of praise. When the doxology is so used I feel that the service never quite recovers from the *faux pas*. An opening hymn should take a lower level, that the service may ascend and not descend."[115] In other words, the likes of Bishop Ken's "Praise God from whom all blessings flow" ought not to be recited on a full stomach, but reserved, as closely as possible, for the sixty to ninety minutes prior to Sunday brunch!

Seriously, though, Benson's lecture to his assembly represented a plea to the effect that the utterance of the likes of the four "praises" in Ken's lines

---

[113] Long Meter (or Long Measure): see note 77 above.

[114] *Te Deum laudamus* ("We praise Thee, O God"), perhaps the most noted non-Biblical hymn of the Western Church, intended, originally, for daily function as a morning hymn. In the West, the "Te Deum" has been a part of the liturgy since the beginning of the sixth century as a hymn for the Sunday service for matins (the morning hours), prior to the lesson from the Gospel. See Julian, *Dictionary of Hymnology*, 2:1119-1134.

[115] *The Hymnody of the Christian Church* (New York: George H. Doran Company, 1927; rpt. Richmond, Virginia: John Knox Press, 1956): 177. Benson then provided a short list of appropriate hymnodic offerings for the opening of the service: "The earth is hushed in silence"; John Ellerton's "This is the day of light" (1867); Joseph D. Carlyle's "Lord, when we bend before Thy throne" (1802); Andrew Reed's "Spirit divine, attend our prayers " (1829).

function as the emotional high point of the worship service--the concluding scene, or even the denouement, of the religious experience that ought to be generated by and from that service. By the time in which Benson set forth his reactions, the theological controversies originating from and surrounding Ken's Doxology had, essentially, been relegated to denominational and theological history; indeed, even those who continued to disagree with the final line of the piece could easily invoke the principle of public domain and alter the text.

However, academicians and professional hymnologists do not always have the final say in such matters. Professor Benson had held his mind's eye to the upper and middle class "mainstream" Protestant church where, indeed, breakfast and the Sunday newspaper shared the sphere of influence with the Sunday worship service. On the other side of the ecclesiastical tracks, the theological, spiritual, and emotional worlds of American evangelicalism--its preachers and their followers--from the mid-nineteenth century to the present moment, have surveyed a far broader view from that which ranged about the isolated quadrangles of the theological seminaries. Thus, for example, "With admirable punctuality, Mr. Moody[116] made his appearance on the platform at exactly half-past seven, by which time the whole hall was filled. With some abruptness, and in a decidedly provincial accent, he gave out the verse, 'Praise God from whom all blessings flow,' adding, 'All sing; let's praise God for what He's going to do.' The congregation responded heartily, every man and woman appearing to join full-voiced in the doxology. Then followed a brief prayer, after which Mr. Moody

---

[116] Dwight Lyman Moody (1837-1899), a native of Northfield, Massachusetts, and a former shoe salesman on the Boston and Chicago circuits who exchanged the railways of commerce for the sawdust trails of evangelicalism. As early as 1858, Moody had organized the North Market Sabbath School in Chicago. Then, with the musician Ira David Sankey (1840-1908), whom he had met in 1870, he began a series of preaching tours and evangelical campaigns throughout the United States and Great Britain. The event described occurred in the Agricultural Hall at Islington, London, in 1875. For a fairly comprehensive summary of the Moody-Sankey rallies in Britain see Ian Bradley, *Abide with Me: The World of Victorian Hymns* (London: SCM Press, Ltd.; Chicago: GIA Publications, Inc,, 1997): 177-184.

gave out the 100th Psalm, again adding, 'Let all the people sing' and certainly all the people did. It was a fine sight to see that vast assemblage rise, and a treat to hear their powerful unison."[117] Thus emerged the functional duality of Bishop Ken's four-line Doxology: the ability to create, at once, a balance between the conventional notion of liturgical propriety and the "powerful unison" of emotional expression.

9. List of Works Cited and Consulted

A. Primary Sources

The Diary of John Evelyn, ed. William Bray. 2 vols. 1907; rev., 1952; rpt. London: J.M. Dent and Sons, Ltd./Everyman's Library, 1966.

[Ken, Thomas.] *A Manual of Prayers for the Use of the Scholars of Winchester College.* London: Printed for John Martyn, 1674.

The Poetical Works of John and Charles Wesley, ed. George Osborn. 13 vols. London: Wesleyan-Methodist Conference Office, 1868-1872.

Three Hymns. By the Author of the Manual of Prayers for the Use of the Scholars of Winchester College. London: Printed for Ch[arles]. Brome, at the Gun, at the West End of St. Paul's Church, 1694.

Wesley, Charles. *Hymns on God's Everlasting Love. To Which Is Added The Cry of a Reprobate and The Horrible Decree.* Bristol: Printed by Samuel and Felix Farley, 1741.

B. Secondary Sources

Allibone, Samuel Austin. *A Critical Dictionary of English Literature and British and American Authors, Living and Deceased, from the Earliest Accounts to the Latter Half of the Nineteenth Century.* 3 vols. Philadelphia: J. B. Lippincott and Company, 1872-1877.

---

[117] Gerald Parsons (ed.), *Religion in Victorian Britain* (Manchester: Manchester University Press, 1988), 3:275.

Barkley, John M., ed. *Handbook to the Church Hymnary. Third Edition. [1973].* London and Oxford: Oxford University Press, 1979.

Benson, Louis Fitzgerald. *The English Hymn: Its Development and Use in Worship.* New York: George H. Doran and Company, 1915; rpt. Richmond, Virginia: John Knox Press, 1962.

-----. *The Hymnody of the Christian Church.* New York: George H. Doran Company, 1927; rpt. Richmond, Virginia, John Knox Press, 1956.

Biggs, Louis Coutier. *English Hymnology.* London: Mozleys, 1873.

Bradley, Ian. *Abide with Me: The World of Victorian Hymns.* London: SC Press, Ltd, 1997; rpt. Chicago: GIA Publications, 1997.

Briggs, Asa. *A Social History of England.* New York: The Viking Press, 1984.

Brown, Theron, and Hezekiah Butterworth. *The Story of Hymns and Tunes.* New York: American Tract Society, 1906.

Burney, Charles. *A General History of Music, from the Earliest Ages to the Present Period [1797],* ed. Frank Mercer. 2 vols. New York: Dover Publications, Inc., 1957.

Carrington, Charles. *Rudyard Kipling.* London: Macmillan and Company, 1955.

Coote, Stephen. *Royal Survivor: A Life of Charles II.* New York: St. Martin's Press, 2000.

Cross, F.L., and E.A. Livingstone, eds. *The Oxford Dictionary of the Christian Church.* 2nd ed. Oxford and New York: Oxford University Press, 1974.

Currie, Robert, Alan Gilbert, and Lee Horsley. *Churches and Churchgoers. Patterns of Church Growth in the British Isles Since 1700.* Oxford: Clarendon Press, 1977.

Davies, Horton. *Worship and Theology in England. II. From Andewes to Baxter and Fox, 1603-1690.* Princeton, New Jersey: Princeton University Press, 1975; rpt. Grand Rapids, Michigan: William B. Eerdmans Publishing Company, 1996.

Dictionary of National Biography (DNB).

Dictionary of North American Hymnology: A Comprehensive Bibliography and Master Index of Hymns and Hymnals Published in the United States and Canada, 1640-1978, comp. Leonard Ellinwood and Elizabeth Lockwood; ed. Paul R. Powell and Mary Louise Van Dyke. Boston: The Hymn Society of the United States and Canada, Inc., 2003. CD-ROM for Windows and Mackintosh.

Eagle, Dorothy, and Hillary Carnall. *The Oxford Literary Guide to the British Isles.* Oxford: At the Clarendon Press, 1977.

Fairchild, Hoxie Neale. *Religious Trends in English Poetry. Volume I. 1700-1740. Protestantism and the Cult of Sentiment.* New York: Columbia University Press, 1939.

Grove's Dictionary of Music and Musicians, 3rd ed., ed. H.C. Coles. 7 vols. New York: The Macmillan Company, 1944.

Hartnoll, Phyllis, ed. *The Oxford Companion to the Theatre.* 3rd ed. London and New York: Oxford University Press, 1967.

Hazen, Allen T. *A Catalogue of Horace Walpole's Library.* 3 vols. New Haven: Yale University Press, 1969.

Julian, John, ed. *A Dictionary of Hymnology. Setting forth the Origin and History of Christian Hymns of All Ages and Nations.* 2nd ed., rev. 2 vols. London: John Murray, 1907; rpt. New York: Dover Publications, Inc., 1957.

Keating, Peter. *Kipling the Poet.* London: Secker and Warburg, 1994.

Kennedy, Michael. *The Oxford Dictionary of Music.* Oxford and New York: Oxford University Press, 1985.

Lewis, Donald M., ed. *The Blackwell Dictionary of Evangelical Biography, 1730-1860.* 2 vols. Oxford: Blackwell Publishers, 1995.

Miller, Madeleine S., and J. Lane Miller. *Harper's Bible Dictionary.* New York: Harper and Brothers, Publishers, 1955.

The New Grove's Dictionary of Music and Musicians. 6th ed. ed. Stanley Sadie. 20 vols. London: Macmillan Publishers, Ltd., 1980.

Northcott, Cecil. *Hymns in Christian Worship. The Use of Hymns in the Life of the Church*. Richmond, Virginia: John Knox Press, 1964.

Ousby, Ian. *Literary Britain and Ireland*. 2nd ed. London: A. and C. Black, Ltd.; New York: W.W. Norton and Company, Inc., 1985.

Parsons, Gerald (ed.). *Religion in Victorian Britain*. Manchester: Manchester University Press, 1988.

Partridge, Eric, ed. *A Classical Dictionary of the Vulgar Tongue. By Captain Francis Grose*. 3rd ed., 1796. New York: Barnes and Noble, Inc, 1963.

-----. *A Dictionary of Slang and Unconventional English*, 5th ed. New York: The Macmillan Company, 1961.

Plomer, Henry R., *A Dictionary of the Printers and Booksellers Who were at Work in England, Scotland, and Ireland from 1668 to 1725*. Oxford: Oxford University Press, 1922; rpt. London: The Bibliographical Society, 1968.

Roberts, Richard Owen. *Whitefield in Print. A Bibliographic Record of Works By, For, and Against George Whitefield*. Wheaton, Illinois: Richard Owen Roberts, Publishers, 1988.

Rogal, Samuel J. *A Biographical Dictionary of Eighteenth-Century Methodism*. 10 vols. Lewiston, New York: The Edwin Mellen Press, 1997-1999.

Routley, Erik. *Hymns and the Faith*. London: John Murray, 1955.

-----. *The Musical Wesleys*. London: Herbert Jenkins, 1968.

Seaborne, Malcolm. *The English School: Its Architecture and Organization, 1370-1870*. Toronto: University of Toronto Press, 1971.

Trager, James, ed. *The People's Chronology: Year-by-Year Record of Human Events, from Prehistory to the Present*. New York: Holt, Rinehart and Winston, 1979.

Trevelyan, George Macaulay. *Illustrated English Social History. Volume Four: The Nineteenth Century.* 1942; rpt. Harmondsworth, Middlesex: Penguin Books, Ltd., 1964.

Tyerman, Luke. *The Life and Times of the Rev. John Wesley, M.A., Founder of the Methodists.* 3 vols. New York: Harper and Brothers, 1872.

-----. *The Life and Times of the Rev. Samuel Wesley, A.M., Rector of Epworth.* London: Simpkin, Marshall and Company, Ltd., 1866.

Weinreb, Ben, and Christopher Hibbert. *The London Encyclopaedia.* 1993; rpt. Bethesda, Maryland: Adler and Adler, Publishers, 1986.

Welsh, R.E., and F.G. Edwards. *Romance of Psalter and Hymnal: Authors and Composers.* London: Hodder and Stoughton, 1889.

C. Hymnals

African American Heritage Hymnal. Chicago: GIA Publications, Inc., 2001.

Appendix to the Psalms and Hymns. London: Society for the Promotion of Christian Knowledge, 1869.

The Book of Praise. Toronto, Ontario: Oxford University Press, 1918.

The Book of Praise. n.p.: The Presbyterian Church in Canada, 1997.

Book of Worship for United States Forces: A Collection of Hymns and Worship Resources for Military Personnel of the United States of America. [Washington, D.C.:] The Armed Forces Chaplains Board, 1974.

The Broadman Hymnal, ed. B.B. McKinney. Nashville: The Broadman Press, 1940.

The Celebration Hymnal. Songs and Hymns for Worship. n.p.: Word Music/Integrity Music, 1997.

Christian Science Hymnal. Boston: The Christian Science Publishing Society, 1932.

Christian Worship. A Hymnal, ed. B. Fred Wise. Philadelphia and St. Louis: Judson Press/Bethany Press, 1941.

Church Book, for the Use of Evangelical Lutheran Congregations. By the Authority of the General Council of the Evangelical Lutheran Church in America. With Music. ed. Harriet Reynolds Krauth. Philadelphia: J.K. Shryock, 1897.

A Church Hymn Book for the United Church of England and Ireland. Toronto, Ontario: Henry Rowsell, 1861.

The Church Hymnal with Canticles, ed. Charles L. Hutchins. Boston: The Parish Choir, 1890.

Church Pastorals, ed. Nehemiah Adams. Boston: Ticknor and Fields, 1864.

Church Psalmody: A Collection of Psalms and Hymns Adapted to Public Worship. Selected from Dr. [Isaac] Watts and Other Authors. Boston: Perkins and Marvin, 1841.

Church Service Hymns. A Superior Collection of Hymns and Gospel Songs, comp. Homer Rodeheaver, George W. Sanville, B.D. Ackley. Winona Lake, Indiana: Rodeheaver Company, 1948.

Devotional Hymns. A Collection of Hymns and Songs for Use in All Services of the Church. Chicago: Hope Publishing Company, 1947.

The English Hymnal with Tunes. Oxford: The University Press, 1906.

The Evangelical Hymnal with Tunes, ed. Charles Cuthbert Hall and Sigismond Lasar. New York and Chicago: A.S. Barnes and Company, 1880.

Evangelical Lutheran Hymnal. Published by Order of the Evangelical Lutheran Joint Synod of Ohio and Other States. 9th ed. Columbus, Ohio: The Lutheran Book Concern, 1910(?)

Favorite Hymns of Praise. Wheaton, Illinois: Tabernacle Publishing Company, 1967, 1973.

Gospel Hymns Nos. 1 to 6 Complete, Excelsior Edition, ed. Ira David Sankey, James McGranahan, and George G. Stebbins. New York and Chicago: The Biglow and Main Company; Cincinnati, New York, and Chicago: The

John Church Company, 1895.

Harmonia Sacra; or, Divine Hymns and Dialogues. . .Composed by the Best Masters. . .The Words by Several Learned and Pious Persons. The Second. Book. London: Henry Playford, 1693..

The Harvard University Hymn Book. 4th ed. Cambridge, Massachusetts; London, England: Harvard University Press, 2007.

Hymnal and Liturgies of the Moravian Church (Unitas Fratrum). Bethlehem, Pennsylvania: Published by Authority of the Provincial Synod, 1920.

The Hymnal. As Authorized and Approved for Use by the General Convention of the Protestant Episcopal Church in the United States of America. New York: The Church Pension Fund, 1933.

The Hymnal Companion to the Book of Common Prayer, 3rd ed., rev. and enl. , ed. Edward Henry Bickersteth. London: Longmans, Green and Company, 1890.

The Hymnal. Containing Complete Orders of Worship. St. Louis: Eden Publishing House, 1941.

The Hymnal of the Evangelical Church. Word Edition. St. Louis: Eden Publishing House, 1900.

Hymnal of the Methodist Episcopal Church. With Tunes. New York: Hunt and Eaton; Cincinnati: Cranston and Stowe, 1878, 1889.

Hymnal of the Protestant Episcopal Church in the United States. New York: The Church Pension Fund, 1940.

The Hymnal. Published by Authority of the General Assembly of the Presbyterian Church in the United States of America. Philadelphia: Presbyterian Board of Christian Education, 1933.

Hymns Ancient and Modern: For Use in the Services of the Church: With Annotations, Originals, References, Authors' and Translators' Names, and with Some Metrical Translations of the Hymns in Latin and German, ed. Louis Coutier Biggs. London: Novello and Company, 1867.

Hymns Ancient and Modern, For Use in the Services of the Church. With Accompanying Tunes. Historical Edition. London: William Ckowes and Sons, Limited, 1909.

The Hymns for the Use of Evangelical Lutheran Congregations. Charleston, South Carolina: Committee of the United Synod on the Common Book of Worship, 1906.

Hymns for the Worship of God, Selected and Arranged for the Use of Congregations Connected with the Presbyterian Church in Canada, ed. Francis Nicol. Montreal, Quebec: John Lovell, 1863.

Hymns of the Christian Life. rev. ed. Harrisburg, Pennsylvania: Christian Publications, 1978.

The Lutheran Hymnal. Authorized by the Synods Constituting the Evangelical Lutheran Synodical Conference of North America. St. Louis: Concordia Publishing House, 1941.

A Manual of Prayers for the Use of the Scholars of Winchester College. And All Other Devout Christians. To Which Is Added Three Hymns for Morning, Evening and Midnight. London: Printed for Charles Brome, 1695; newly revised. London: Printed for Charles Brome, 1709.

The Methodist Hymn Book, Revised and Approved: Designated As a Constant Companion for the Pious of All Denominations. Forty-Fifth Edition. New York: Published by J. Soule and T. Mason for the Methodist Episcopal Church in the United States, 1818.

The Methodist Hymnal. Official Hymnal of the Methodist Church. Nashville: The Methodist Publishing House, 1966.

The Methodist Hymnal. Official Hymnal of the Methodist Episcopal Church, The , Methodist Episcopal Church South, The Methodist Protestant Church. New York, Cincinnati, and Chicago: The Methodist Book Concern, 1935.

The National Baptist Hymn Book. A Collection of Old Meter Songs. 4th ed. ed. R.H. Boyd. Nashville: National Baptist Publishing Board, 1906.

A New Hymnal for Colleges and Schools, ed. Jeffery Rowthorn and Russell Schulz-Widmar. New Haven and London : Yale University Press/Yale Institute of Sacred Music, 1992.

The Praise Hymnary, ed. T.J. Morgan, W.A. May, and Phoebe Haynes, Boston, New York, and Chicago: Silver Burdett and Company, 1898.

The Psalmist: A New Collection of Hymns for the Use of the Baptist Churches, ed. Baron Stow and Samuel Francis Smith. Boston: Gould and Lincoln, 1854.

The Psalms and Hymns, with the Catechism, Confession of Faith, and Canons of the Synod of Dort, and Liturgy of the Reformed Protestant Dutch Church in North America. Philadelphia: The General Synod, 1854.

Psalms, Hymns, and Spiritual Songs of the Rev. Isaac Watts, D.D., to Which Are Added, Select Hymns from Other Authors, ed. Samuel Worcester. New Edition, ed. Samuel M. Worcester. Boston: Crocker and Brewster, 1834.

Psalms, Hymns and Spiritual Songs: Selected and Original, Designed for Use of the Church Universal, ed. George Richards and Oliver W. Lane. Boston: I. Thomas and T.E. Andrews, 1792.

The Sabbath Hymn Book. For the Service of Song in the House of the Lord, ed. Edwards Amassa Park and Austin Phelps. New York: Mason Brothers, 1858.

Selection of Hymns from the Best Authors, Intended As an Appendix to Dr. [Isaac] Watts' Psalms and Hymns, ed. John Rippon. American Edition. New York: William Durrell, 1792.

Serum Corda, ed. Elias Henry Johnson. Philadelphia: American Baptist Publication Society, 1898.

Service Book and Hymnal, Authorized by the [Lutheran] Churches Cooperating in the Commission on the Liturgy and Hymnal. Minneapolis: Augsburg Publishing House; Philadelphia: Fortress Press, 1958.

Services of Religion for Use in the Churches of the Free Spirit. Boston: The Beacon Press, Inc., 1937.

Sing to the Lord. Hymnal. Kansas City, Missouri: Lillenas Publishing Company, 1993.

The Springfield Collection of Hymns for Sacred Worship, ed. William Bourne Oliver Peabody. Springfield, Massachusetts: Samuel Bowles, 1835.

The Sunday School Hymnal. Edition "D," ed. Charles L. Hutchins. Boston: Congregational Publishing House, 1871.

The United Methodist Hymnal. Book of United Methodist Worship. Nashville: The United Methodist Publishing House, 1989.

University Hymns, ed. Harry Benjamin Jepson and Charles Reynolds Brown. New Haven: Yale University Press, 1924.

Warrior Songs for the White Cavalry, ed. Frank W. Sandford. 3rd ed. Boston: The Kingdom Publishing Company, 1951.

Wartburg Hymnal, for Church, School, and Home. Ed. O. Hardwig. Chicago: Wartburg Publishing House, 1918.

Worship His Majesty. Alexandria, Indiana: Gaither Music Company, Inc., 1987.

The Worshiping Church. A Hymnal. Carol Stream, Illinois: Hope Publishing Company, 1990.

Wren, Brian. *Faith Looking Forward: The Hymns and Songs of Brian Wren. With Many Tunes by Peter Cutts*. Carol Stream, Illinois: Hope Publishing Company, 1983.

HISTORY OF CHRISTIAN HYMNODY

1. Samuel J. Rogal, *Praise God from Whom All Blessings Flow*: A Sung Prayer of the Christian Tradition

2. Nancy James, *In Your Mercy, Lord, You Called Me* : A Sung Prayer in the Christian Tradition

3. Charles Parsons, *Pange Lingua*: A Sung Prayer of the Christian Tradition

4. Samuel J. Rogal, *Eternal Father, Strong to Save*: A Sung Prayer of the Christian Tradition

5. Robert B. Pierce, *A Stable-Lamp is Lighted*: A Sung Prayer of the Christian Tradition

6. Samuel J. Rogal, *All Hail the Power of Jesus' Name*: A Sung Prayer of the Christian Tradition

7. Samuel J. Rogal, *Recessional: A Victorian Ode (God of Our Fathers, Known of Old*: A Sung Prayer of the Christian Tradition

8. Samuel J. Rogal, *Rock of Ages, Cleft for Me*: A Sung Prayer of the Christian Tradition

9. Samuel J. Rogal, *Abide With Me, Fast Falls the Eventide*: A Sung Prayer of the Christian Tradition

10. Samuel J. Rogal, *O For a Thousand Tongues to Sing*: A Sung Prayer of the Christian Tradition

11. Samuel J. Rogal, *Onward Christian Soldiers*: A Sung Prayer of the Christian Tradition

Samuel J. Rogal

Dr. Samuel Rogal (Emeritus) was the Chair of the Division of Humanities and Fine Arts at Illinois Valley Community College, Oglesby, Illinois. The author of many books and articles, he has published several specialized monographs on John Wesley with The Edwin Mellen Press, including *John Wesley's London: A Guidebook* (1988); *John Wesley's Mission to Scotland, 1751-1790* (1989); *John Wesley in Ireland* (1993); and *John Wesley in Wales, 1739-1790* (1995). He also compiled a well-received reference set, the 10-volume *Biographical Dictionary of 18th-Century Methodism* (The Edwin Mellen Press, 1997-2000).

www.ingramcontent.com/pod-product-compliance
Lightning Source LLC
Chambersburg PA
CBHW021003230426
43666CB00005B/266